Our ivy is in a league by itself.

RHODES

COLLEGE

PHOTOGRAPHED BY WILLIAM STRODE

HARMONY HOUSE
Publishers Louisville

Peyton Nalle Rhodes
1900-1984
President of the College, 1949-1965, whose
name the College adopted on July 1, 1984.
"By their action the Trustees have
chosen to link the spirit of this
college with the inspiration of the
man who has helped to give it
life for over half a century."

We wish to thank the Rhodes College Community for its help
in the production of this book, and in particular President
James H. Daughdrill Jr. and Loyd Templeton, Assistant to the President
for College Relations, for their dedication to the project. Special thanks
also to Helen Norman and Sheila Dailey for their valuable efforts. Finally,
for his many hours of research and photographic help in the Archives,
we wish to thank Mr. Goodbar Morgan.

Executive Editors: William Butt and William Strode
Library of Congress Catalog number 85-081583
Hardcover International Standard Book Number 0-916509-03-6
Printed in USA by Pinaire Lithographing Corp., Louisville, Kentucky
First Edition printed 1985 by Harmony House Publishers—Louisville,
Box 90, Prospect, Kentucky 40059. (502) 228-2010/228-4446.
Copyright © 1985 by Harmony House Publishers—Louisville
Photographs copyright © by William Strode

INTRODUCTION

by James E. Roper
Charles E. Glover Professor of English Studies

It all began 23,000 years ago with a conscientious mastodon who carefully chose his spot to become extinct. When the dragline excavating for the biology building uncovered his bones, he was off target a little and in the way of a planned drinking fountain. But his tusks formed a proper kind of pointed arch, so he was enshrined in a glass coffin just a few feet away as the earliest example of Gothic architecture on campus.

As these pages reveal, at Rhodes College the brown-orange stone is absolute. The man responsible for all this integrity of quality and style was Charles Edward Diehl. If, as alleged, architecture is frozen music, then the college is his battle hymn against expediency and mediocrity.

When he came to stand under John Fargason's great oaks, part of a virgin forest shared with Overton Park and just presented to him as a portion of the hundred-acre campus donated by Memphis and certain of its citizens, he knew exactly what he wanted to do with it:

Here was the chance of a lifetime; a chance to set the standards of an institution for all time; a chance to go forth unhampered by past mistakes, architectural and other, and to launch an institution which was as nearly ideal for its purpose as painstaking investigation and careful thought could make it. Realizing that the good is ever the enemy of the best, we did not seek merely the good, but the best. There was ever before us the ideal of excellence. It was our purpose to launch here an institution that would endure for centuries, and that would command the respect and quicken the pride of succeeding generations.

The permanency and continuity of a college rest not only on the enduring stone and the people who plan and change and teach and maintain, but also on less tangible things such as the spirit that moves through the memories of alumni, catching on a hook of the mind here and there, and fluttering for a moment in the breezes of affection. It makes its strongest epiphanies only at homecoming or other nostalgic occasions, and its vignettes may not make the color plates, but its gossamer has the binding force of epoxy. Each graduate has an individual cluster of these living memories that lets him know he is part of some living organism that has, by a strange symbiosis, become a permanent part of him in turn.

At Rhodes these wisps might be things like Wesley Halliburton at the age of ninety-two riding the workmen's hoist daily to the top of his tower to make sure every stone was perfectly placed...the spotlight on the east end of Palmer Hall fixing its beam on the doorway of the only women's dorm then, as a response to a petition from unescorted residents, only to be blasted as Big Brother at work by those

who had dates and preferred the dark for lingering goodnights...the professor dealing with unshod medieval friars in the snow and scorning modern wimpiness, only to be greeted soon after by forty waving bare feet dripping the first snowfall all over his classroom floor...the women swathed in raincoats so they could go to phys-ed in their gym shorts, after which they strolled the campus in mini-skirts shorter by far...springtime impulses in that benighted era before Fort Lauderdale, sweeping the young man's fancy into that bizarre quest, the panty raid, in which the seeker seems to prefer the samite covering to the grail itself...the once-complete "S" of oaks on the front campus, planted as acorns brought from Clarksville and now not only imperfect but irrelevant... the transgressing freshmen in their beanies counting the slates of Palmer terrace with a brick in each hand...All these are the special associations that make the alumnus or alumna muse where the detached viewer sees only what he sees.

And the secrets, hallmarks of the inner circle of those who care, the cicatrice or mole that only the intimate lover knows and values...the room in Frazier-Jelke basement sealed off like a pharaoh's tomb, where construction went awry and the space could not be made available for use because the blue-prints denied its existence...the fact that the physics tower is not planned by an architect, but by an ex-Navy man who thought of it as an aircraft carrier with its "island" of service units and its "deck" of classrooms and labs...that President Rhodes' office was called "Peyton Place"...that the superb proportions of the Halliburton Tower are based on the Fibonacci number series that mysteriously links the arts and sciences, the works of nature and the works of man, the "golden section" that gives perfection to the Parthenon or Mondrian's rectangles or the facade of Notre Dame in Paris, and the spiral curve of the snail shell or the chambers of the nautilus or the number of seed rows in a sunflower head.

And the Great Two-Headed Secret, summed up in the two inscriptions carved into bronze on each side of the majestic bell, which few are aware of and which fewer still will ever gaze upon. Between them they give a fairly good capsule version of the liberal arts education at its best. On commencement day, as the armed and eager graduates head up the aisle with their parchment swords in hand, the five-ton oracle in the Tower bongs on one side to share and incite the up-and-at-'em joy of these freed individuals; the vibrations circle out from the words, *The day shall not be up so soon as I/To share the fair adventure of tomorrow.* And then it bongs back to the other side to give sober warning that the dragons of success and wealth lie in wait for the unwary, and admonishes in darker tones to usher the departing senior off the campus,

Not fare well,
But fare forward, voyagers.

Rhodes Historical Resume

1848 Founding of the Masonic University of Tennessee

1855 Purchase of Masonic University by the Synod of Nashville

1869 Reopening of the college after it had been closed during the Civil War

1875 Name changed to Southwestern Presbyterian University

1878 Establishment of Greek-letter fraternities

1884 Dr. Joseph R. Wilson named Head of the new School of Theology.

1904 $25,000 paid by the Federal Government for damages sustained during the Civil War

1916 Board decides to admit women as students

1917 Dr. Charles E. Diehl named President

1918 The Honor System established

1919 SOU'WESTER began publication

1920 Approval of the four controlling synods of a plan for removal of the University to Memphis

1922 Sororities established

1924 Name of the college changed to Southwestern

1925 College opened in Memphis
Jubilee Celebration

1927 ODK National Honorary Leadership Fraternity established

1928 Honors courses introduced

1930 Mortgage indebtedness of $700,000 retired

1931 Charges of heresy brought against Dr. Diehl
Tutorial system established

1935 Department of Music established

1936 Southwestern Singers organized

1941 Hubert F. Fisher Memorial Garden provided

1943 Southwestern selected for training of ASTP cadets

1944 Adult Education offered

1945 Groundbreaking (1945) and completion (1946) of Voorhies Hall
The "Man" course introduced
Name changed to Southwestern At Memphis

1947 Dedication of Gordon White Hall

1949 Establishment of Phi Beta Kappa Chapter
Inauguration of Peyton N. Rhodes and Centennial Celebration

1950 Bellingrath-Morse Foundation and Jessie L. Clough Art Memorial for Teaching established

1953 Dedication of Burrow Library

1954 Dedication of Neely Mallory Memorial Gymnasium

1955 Ford Foundation Grant received
International Studies program formed

1956 Dedication of Ellett Hall
The Kinney Program begun

1958 Dedication of Catherine Burrow Refectory
The Language Center established

1961 Dedication of Bellingrath Hall
Dedication of Townsend Hall

1962 College Athletic Conference chartered
Dedication of Moore Moore Infirmary
Dedication of Richard Halliburton Memorial Tower

1964 Formation of the Laboratory of Atmospheric and Optical Physics

1965 Challenge grant by Ford Foundation offered

1966 Dilemma Symposium initiated
Dedication of Suzanne Trezevant Hall
Dedication of Thomas W. Briggs Student Center
Inauguration of John David Alexander

1968 Dedication of Alfred C. Glassell Hall

Dedication of Frazier-Jelke Science Center, Kennedy Chemistry Hall and the Buckman Library

1969 Groundbreaking (1969) and dedication (1970) of S. DeWitt Clough Hall of Fine Arts and Humanities

1970 Inauguration of William L. Bowden

Southwestern at Oxford established

1971 Dedication of Ruth Sherman Hyde Memorial Gymnasium for Women

1972 A. Van Pritchartt appointed interim president

1973 Inauguration of James H. Daughdrill, Jr.

Budget balanced

1974 Change in makeup of the controlling synods of Southwestern

1975 Golden Anniversary of opening in Memphis

1976 Frank E. Seidman Distinguished Award in Political Economy Program and M. L. Seidman lectures established

1977 $20 Million Commitment Campaign begun

Dedication of Alburty Swimming Pool

1978 The Harry B. McCoy, Jr. Visiting Artists Program established

Thirteen buildings named historic sites by the National Register of Historic Places

1980 Gooch Bequest—largest single gift ($2 million) to date in the history of the College

Dedication of the Anne Marie Caskey Williford Hall

Abe Plough Gift—Fund established as a perpetual source of tuition scholarships for Southwestern students

Dedication of the Falls Austin Building

New computer system installed

1981 Clarence Day Awards for Teaching established

Rhodes Tower (Physics) dedicated

Gooch Hall dedicated

1982 McCoy Theatre dedicated

1983 Bellingrath, Goodrich, Hyde Merit Scholarships established

Diehl Memorial and LeMaster Gateway dedicated

1984 Board of Trustees meeting, Grand Hotel, Point Clear, Alabama

At this important Board of Trustees meeting Rhodes College is committed to being one of the finest colleges of liberal arts and sciences in the nation

Hassell Hall (Music Building) dedicated

First fully endowed professorship established (Buckman Family-Buckman Laboratories, Inc.)

Southwestern Board of Trustees meets to vote on changing the name of College to Rhodes College—vote was unanimous

East Residence Hall groundbreaking

Southwestern at Memphis became Rhodes College (July 1, 1984)

The Lillian and Morrie Moss Endowment for the Visual Arts established

Dr. Peyton N. Rhodes died

1985 Dedication of Benefactors' Circle in the Cloister of Palmer Hall

East Residence Hall opened

Announcement that College benefactors have committed $75 million during the first 8 years of the College's Ten-Year Development Campaign.

*Appropriate and beautiful surroundings
will have a transforming influence upon
generation after generation of students and
upon the very character of the institution
itself. Beauty, like Truth and Goodness,
needs but to be expressed.*
Charles E. Diehl

*Therefore when we build, let us think that
we build forever. Let it not be for present
use alone; let it be such work as our
descendants will thank us for, and let us
think, as we lay stone on stone, that a time
is to come when those stones will be held
sacred because our hands have touched
them, and that men will say as they look
upon the labor and wrought substance of
them, "See! This our fathers did for us."*
Ruskin

The Charles E. Diehl Memorial; the cast bronze sculpture is by the eminent artist Edwin Rust.

The time will never come when the teacher is not the most important part of the college. He is the college in the active sense; all other things are circumstances, machinery, arrangements. He is the mind that learns and teaches. If he does well, then all is well.
Bulletin, 1925

Windows in the Williams Prayer Room of Voohries Hall

I go for stone gothic, rubble wall, crevices for moss and ivy, holes where old time may stick in his memorials.
Ruskin

East Residence Hall

Berthold S. Kennedy Hall

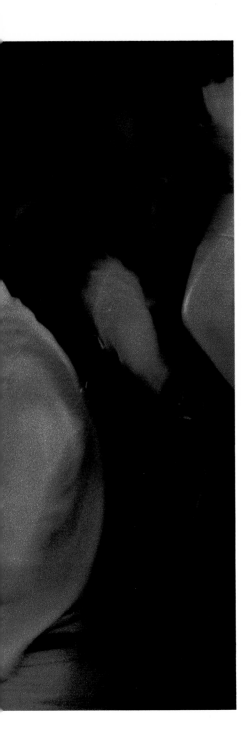

Overleaf: Rhodes Physics Tower Observatory

53

Despite the changes in the times, and they have been drastic, the College has remained essentially the same. It has remained the same because it is built on timeless truths and ideals.
W. T. Pearson, '23, at Commencement, 1948

The original bell from the Clarksville campus hangs above the entrance to the Catherine Burrow Refectory.

With the campus located only minutes from downtown Memphis, Rhodes students enjoy the amenities of a major city as well as the benefits of their own college community.

Realizing that the good is ever the enemy of the best, we did not seek merely the good but the best. There was ever before us the ideal of excellence.
Charles E. Diehl

*Palmer Hall, dedicated November, 1925, is one
of 13 campus buildings named to the National
Register of Historic Places.*

The Buckman Library, Mathematics Building

Over the portals of the Burrow Library are emblazoned the symbols of the original seven liberal arts.

And so we are here tonight in the presence
of a sermon in soaring stone with its great,
deep, mellow bell...
Peyton Rhodes, Halliburton Memorial
Tower dedication, 1962

The college holds aloft the unpurchasables as the objects of desire and bears an un-faltering testimony to the value of spiritual ideals.
Charles E. Diehl

Catherine Burrow Refectory

*Of course every man's Alma Mater has an appeal to him that
he thinks is unique, but I am convinced that there is something
unusually impelling about the appeal the College makes to her
former students. The atmosphere of the College has always been
such that men and women have felt a mystic influence tugging
at their heart strings, pleading for another day within her walls.*
Rev. William Crowe, '21. Alumni Day 1931

One of the greatest upsets ever to happen in Dudley Stadium occurred Saturday afternoon as the Vanderbilt Commodores, rated as a three to five touchdown favorite, were jolted by the Lynx from Memphis...It's not just the whole town. It's not just the whole South. It's the whole football world that's talking about the epoch-making upset.
The Memphis Commercial-Appeal, 1936

Mr. Rhodes

presented to

Raymond A. Fields III

at Homecoming on this twelfth
of October in the year nineteen
hundred eighty-five for outstanding
contributions to the community
of Rhodes College

PRESIDENT

Ms. Rhodes

presented to

Wheeler Hughes

on this twelfth
in the year nineteen

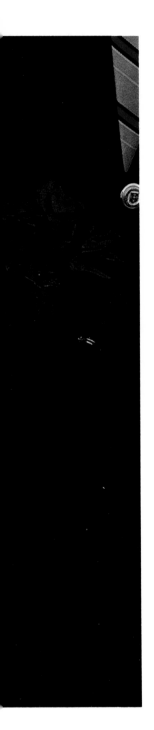

Idlewild Presbyterian Church is the setting of Rhodes' annual Baccalaureate Service.

"The day will not be up so soon as I,
to try the fair adventure of tomorrow."
Shakespeare, inscription on the Halliburton bell

*The purpose of Rhodes College
is to educate students to lead
lives of genuineness and excellence,
to expand the horizons of knowledge and
scholarship, and to live as a community of
truth, loyalty and service.*
President James H. Daughdrill Jr.,
Mission Statement, 1984

*We who drank in knowledge
as students, who acquired a moral and mental and physical stamp
that shall endure, we who are alumni—we owe her much.*
Richard A. Bolling, '10 in Alumni Magazine, 1928

A LOOK AT RHODES COLLEGE IN THE PAST

"In books lies the soul of the whole Past Time, the articulate audible voice of the Past, when the body and material substance of it has altogether vanished like a dream."

Thomas Carlyle

The "Castle" on the Clarksville campus. The stone shield abote the doorway has the names of the 15 founders inscribed. The shield has since been moved to the south face of the Halliburton Tower. The wing to the right of the doorway housed the Physics Department. The bay just left of the door was a biology lab of Dr. Marion MacQueen's. Fraternities met on the upper stories.

Southwestern Presbyterian University in Clarksville, Tennessee ca. 1918. Left to right, buildings are identified as: The Castle, Stewart Hall, The Commons, Calvin Hall, the President's home, and Robb Hall.

This group of faculty members posed for
a picture in 1884.

Joseph R. Wilson, professor of Theology and Homiletics at Southwestern, and father of Woodrow Wilson, former President of the United States.

The starting eleven on Southwestern's 1919 football team, identified as: top, left to right, Robinson, Lindamood, Cobb and Moore; bottom row, Ayres, McAtee, Grizzard, McReynolds, Downing, Ferguson, Culberson.

An airview of 1927 shows the progress of buildings and athletic fields. Palmer Hall is at left.

If you drove through the entrance to the campus from North Parkway in 1930 this is the view you would have. Palmer Hall is on right.

Students of Southwestern Colle
sembled for the opening of the insti
second year in Memphis.
—Ph   e by

As I looked at Palmer Hall with its attendant memorials with enjoyable admiration and wonder, the same thought came to me that possessed me when I said goodbye to the Masonic College in 1854:
I am looking at a perpetuity.
T. H. Elliot, Class of 1885

Palmer Hall, just after construction ca. 1925. This building is one of 13 campus buildings added to the National Register of Historic Places in 1978.

England's Lord and Lady Halifax visit the
Rhodes campus during World War II.

The 13th College Training Detachment
(Aircrew) was stationed at Rhodes during
the war years. Here the men march in front
of Palmer Hall in 1944.

Beauty contest at Rhodes in 1951 brings out 13 co-eds. Front row, left to right: Elizabeth Carr, Anne Feemster, Peggy Crocker, Marilyn Mitchell, Anne Hebert, Margaret Jones, Beverly Mayhall. Back row: Sara Jane Bryant, Claudia Owen, Ester Jane Swartzfager, Barbara Mann, Rebecca Spencer.

The Cloister between classes in the '50s.

Cheerleaders in 1952 included Marzette Smith, Millie Bunn, Mary Rodriguez, Charlie Andrews, Chandler Warren, Elizabeth Carter and Lindsay Stephenson.

Post-war activities on campus included the famous Pajama Race. Here, freshmen in 1949 assemble on the football field before the race.

Neely Hall's lower level housed the Lynx Lair
for many years, shown here in the late 1940's.

Students in 1953 gather at the Lynx Lair.

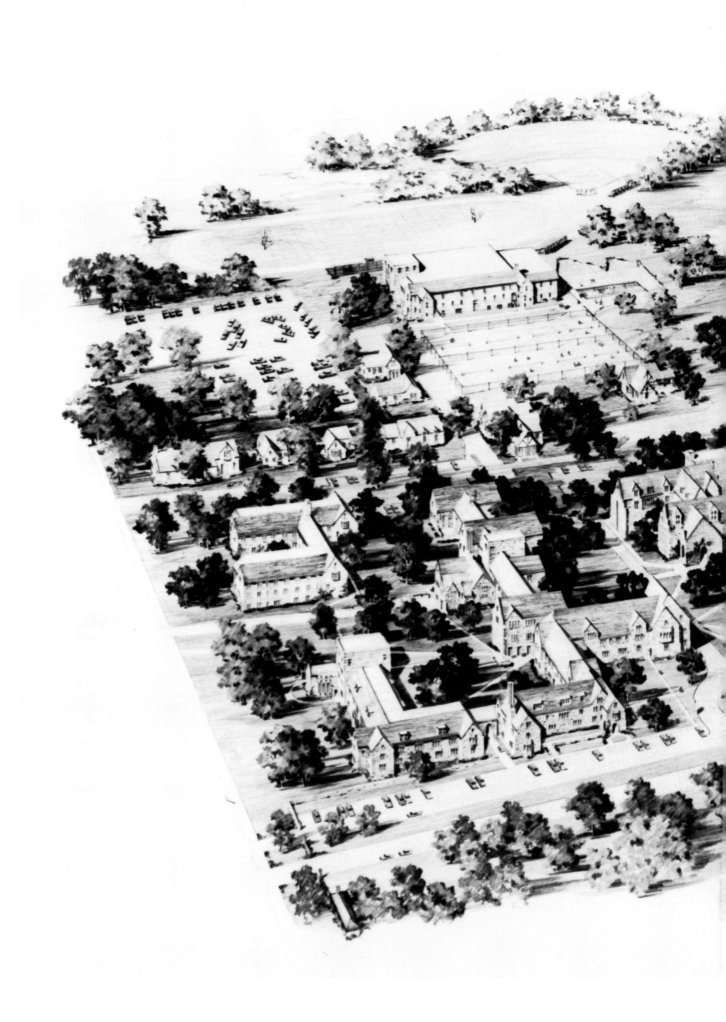